Undeniable Connections

My Adoption Story of Sacrificial Love and Redemption

Linda Beggs

WESTBOW
PRESS®

A DIVISION OF THOMAS NELSON
& ZONDERVAN

Scriptures taken from the Holy Bible, New International Version®, NIV®. Copyright © 1973, 1978, 1984, 2011 by Biblica, Inc.™ Used by permission of Zondervan. All rights reserved worldwide. www.zondervan.com The "NIV" and "New International Version" are trademarks registered in the United States Patent and Trademark Office by Biblica, Inc.™ All rights reserved.

Scripture quotations taken from the Holy Bible, New Living Translation, Copyright © 1996, 2004. Used by permission of Tyndale House Publishers, Inc., Wheaton, Illinois 60189. All rights reserved.

Scripture taken from the King James Version of the Bible.

Some scripture quotations in this publications are from The Message. Copyright © by Eugene H. Peterson 1993, 1994, 1995, 1996, 2000, 2001, 2002. Used by permission of NavPress Publishing Group.

Scripture quotations taken from the New American Standard Bible®, Copyright © 1960, 1962, 1963, 1968, 1971, 1972, 1973, 1975, 1977, 1995 by The Lockman Foundation. Used by permission. (www.Lockman.org)

Cover art by Christine K. Photography

WestBow Press books may be ordered through booksellers or by contacting:

WestBow Press
A Division of Thomas Nelson & Zondervan
1663 Liberty Drive
Bloomington, IN 47403
www.westbowpress.com
1 (866) 928-1240

Because of the dynamic nature of the Internet, any web addresses or links contained in this book may have changed since publication and may no longer be valid. The views expressed in this work are solely those of the author and do not necessarily reflect the views of the publisher, and the publisher hereby disclaims any responsibility for them.

Any people depicted in stock imagery provided by Thinkstock are models, and such images are being used for illustrative purposes only. Certain stock imagery © Thinkstock.

ISBN: 978-1-5127-0093-0 (sc)
ISBN: 978-1-5127-0095-4 (hc)
ISBN: 978-1-5127-0094-7 (e)

Print information available on the last page.

WestBow Press rev. date: 12/17/2015

Dedicated to

The memory of Pauline, my beautiful and sweet
Southern mother who gave me the gift of life.

The honor of my loving mom and dad who
have been my lifelong cheerleaders.

Also dedicated to:

Gary, my handsome prince who believes
in me and sacrificially loves me.
Calle', my precious daughter.
Charles, my charmer.
Chrissy, my princess.
Tim, a loving son whom I've adopted in my heart.

And to God, the lover of my soul.

This story is true.
It was written to offer hope,
encouragement, and peace for all of those with
undeniable connections.

—Linda Beggs

Contents

Legacy of an Adopted Child

—Author Unknown

Once there were two women
Who never knew each other;
One you do not remember,
The other you call mother.

One gave you a nationality,
The other gave you a name;
One gave you the seed of talent,
The other gave you an aim.

Two different lives shaped
To make yours one;
One became your guiding star,
The other became your sun.

One gave you emotions,
The other calmed your fears;
One saw your first sweet smile,
The other dried your tears.

The first gave you life and
The second taught you to live it;
The first gave you a need for love,
And the second was there to give it.

One gave you up,
It was all that she could do;
The other prayed for a child,
And God led her straight to you.

And now you ask me through your tears
The age-old question through the years:
Heredity or environment: Which are you the product of?
Neither, my darling, neither—
Just two different kinds of love.

"For I know the plans I have for you," declares the LORD, "plans to prosper you and not to harm you, plans to give you hope and a future." Jeremiah 29:11 (NIV)

Prologue

As I walked over to my birth mother's casket and laid my hands on it, the grief was overwhelming. Uncontrollable sobs wrenched through my body, matched by a great, deep sorrow. I couldn't leave her graveside. This grief grabbed my soul in such a way that it caught me by surprise, and yet it seemed vaguely familiar. My heart had been broken like this before ... but when? As I cried, I couldn't help but sense the familiarity of this grief deep down in my soul. It wasn't until my husband helped me into our car and we began to drive away that I finally recognized this heartache. I believe that it was the same anguish I experienced when I was taken away from my mother at birth. Could a tiny newborn grieve and mourn for the mother who never held her? Is it possible that this baby would cry for days because the familiar voice and heartbeat that was her world suddenly was gone? I now believe the answer is yes.

CHAPTER 1

A Love Story

*"Three things will last forever —faith, hope, and
love—and the greatest of these is love."*

1 Corinthians 13:13 (NLT)

I t all began in the early months of 1958. My mother, Pauline, was a single working mom with two children. After going through a difficult separation and then divorce, she soon found work. Although her roots were in Tennessee, she was living in central Indiana, trying to work hard enough to support her family. Several of her brothers and sisters lived in that area as well because of job opportunities. She had become very good friends with a man named Woody who frequented the truck stop where she worked as a waitress. Their friendship grew into romance, and she became pregnant with me.

When Pauline brought up the idea of marriage, without revealing her pregnancy, it ended in a heated argument, and he moved away and joined the navy. Since she was barely making ends meet with a two-year-old son and a seven-year-old daughter at home, she had no idea as to what to do. Abortion was never an option because of her upbringing, so she was left alone with a very dark secret that she kept to herself.

My adoptive parents married December 24, 1955, while my mom, Mary, was on Christmas break and my dad, Jack, was in college. My mom was an elementary teacher in Marion, Indiana, and my dad was just finishing up school at Indiana Wesleyan University after being drafted into the army in the middle of his college career. They had always imagined having children in their future.

Mom, who was raised in Chicago, Illinois, had three brothers. She was a natural teacher and loved children. After teaching at an elementary school all day, she was involved in children's clubs and teaching children in Sunday school. My dad, a Michigan native, came from a family of ten siblings. He played a vital role in raising his younger brothers and sisters. In fact, he was given the responsibility of caring for his younger sister, Carol. It was his job to braid her hair each morning and help get her ready for school. He knew how to cook and care for babies, yet took an active role as a teenager helping out with chores at neighboring farms. He also loved children.

After my mom and dad got married, they were anxious to have their first baby. But after unsuccessfully trying to conceive, they sought out a doctor's help. Often during this time, my dad's siblings would tease my parents and ask them if they knew how to make a baby, and my mom and dad were the brunt of many crushing jokes. They never shared their heartache over trying to conceive to anyone but God. They cried out to Him often for a baby they could call their own.

Meanwhile, after finally gathering up enough courage, Pauline made an appointment with her doctor to confirm her pregnancy. Dr. Boyer was a female physician who practiced family medicine in Marion, Indiana, and Pauline seemed drawn to see her. During this visit Pauline poured her heart out to Dr. Boyer and told her about her fears of not being able to financially care for another baby. Because Dr. Boyer was a Christian and had a strong conviction regarding the sanctity of life, abortion was never an option.

Dr. Boyer asked Pauline if she would ever consider putting the baby up for adoption. Pauline began to weep harder, and her body heaved as the doctor told about a couple she was treating and their desire to have a baby. Pauline gathered her composure and began to tell Dr. Boyer that she only wanted her baby to go into a "Christian home" where the child would learn about God. Dr. Boyer told her that this couple loved Jesus and the man was studying to be a pastor.

I think that God must have smiled as His plan came together and arrangements were then made for my private adoption. Dr. Boyer gathered all the necessary information from Pauline, my mom and dad and she told my parents that I would be born in September. My dad finished school in May, and they moved to Kaleva, Michigan, that spring to begin ministry in their first church. Often they would think back to the time when Dr. Boyer told them about a single mother who could not care for the baby she was expecting. They remembered the excitement of hearing how this baby needed a Christian home, their tears of joy as the doctor asked if they would be willing to adopt this baby and their final handshake with Dr. Boyer that sealed their decision to adopt. God had heard their cries and was giving them their hearts' desire!

As the weeks passed, there was no more communication from Dr. Boyer. They wondered if it was because of the distance or if Pauline had changed her mind about the adoption. But, finally, on August 29, 1958, after finishing a refreshing swim in Lake Michigan, my mom and dad received a phone call from Dr. Boyer telling them that their daughter was just born and they needed to make a trip to Marion, Indiana, to pick her up from the hospital. They were shocked and excited all at the same time. After all ... who else but adoptive parents could be swimming while their child was born?

Immediately after my birth, Pauline chose not to see me because she knew that she would not be able to give me up for adoption if she did. So she lay in her hospital bed with empty arms and cried. She said she thought her heart would explode from the sobs that shook her body. I know now that although I left her body, I never left her heart. I also believe that all through my life I still hear her heartbeat and we are somehow connected.

CHAPTER 2

The Formation
of a Family

"Don't you see that children are God's best gift?"

Psalm 127:3a (The Message)

While I grew up, my mom and dad openly shared with me the story of my adoption. They told me how they prayed and asked God for a baby, and God gave them me. As I grew older and asked more questions, they told me about a loving woman, named Pauline, who couldn't take care of her baby. They told me how she gave them the greatest gift of all, her baby to raise.

When I was a young adult, they told me her last name and answered more questions about her. They said she was a beautiful lady who had two young children she was trying to care for while working full-time. They also said that when it came time for her to sign the paperwork to terminate her parental rights, her hands shook and she cried. I couldn't help but think of the great sacrifice she made for my well-being. She sacrificed her desires to mother me so that I could be raised in a loving home and be taught about Jesus. That was her goal ... and my mom and dad didn't let her down.

I had a great childhood. I remember being the princess in our home! When I was three, my mom and dad began praying for another child. Shortly after that they adopted my sister, Laura, into our family. She was six years old and immediately dethroned the three-year-old princess. My earliest memory of her is when she woke me up (which is never a good thing) from my "Princess Nap" on my mom and dad's bed. She proudly announced that she was my new sister and I would have to share half of my toys with her. I remember thinking, *"I didn't ask for a new sister."*

Unfortunately, we never meshed. Laura was beautiful and very petite. She could sing like a lark and captured everyone's heart. Laura also came from a background of abuse and struggled with many issues while growing up. I always wished we could have developed a close relationship but we were always polar opposites. A few years later, after my mom and dad adopted my sister, they decided that they were going to pray more specifically and they asked God for a baby boy. Shortly after that, our family was "considered" for a baby through an adoption agency in Muskegon, Michigan. By then I was six years old, and the thought of a baby brother was very exciting. I remember going to the adoption agency and being interviewed by a man and a woman. They had us assemble puzzles and color pictures, and they asked my sister and me what seemed to be an endless list of questions. The next thing I remember was bringing my baby brother home from the agency. We all wanted to hold him. It was a magical moment, and I loved the way God answered our family's prayer. I embraced the miracle of adoption and loved our new family.

While growing up, we had great birthday celebrations, magical Christmases, and fun family vacations. A special memory I have was our Monday evening "Family Nights." We would do crafts, play games, or go somewhere special. Since my dad was a pastor, we spent a lot of time at church, and I loved it. I remember that my dad would preach about God's love for me and His sacrifice of giving His only Son, Jesus Christ, to die for my sins. When I was five years old, I surrendered my life to Jesus as my dad tenderly explained my need for a Savior. It was the best decision of my life.

I had a brother and a sister, and everything was considered "normal" by our family. However, some things were not. My sister, Laura, was small and petite, and I was huge. I was 5'10" in sixth grade, and my sister was 4'10" in high school. Although I was three years younger than Laura, I towered over her physically, and everyone presumed that I was the older. She struggled academically (I think because of her rough life prior to her adoption), and eventually we ended up in the same grade while in elementary school. I used to love school until I heard a teacher once say to her, "Why can't you get good grades like your sister?" I hated that. Shortly after that episode I would purposely do poorly on tests and papers to take the heat off my sister. There were times when I wanted to protect her because she was my sister, and I hated when people compared us.

Thus began the rivalry between my sister and me. We never chose the competition, but it was there. My sister began to hate me, and she struggled in every area of life. I loved her but I feared her as well. On the other hand, my brother and I have always had a great relationship. He was my baby brother, and in fact, to this very day, although he is in his forties and bald, he is still my baby brother! Even through the struggles with my sister, the joy of my brother, P. D., made everything all right. Our family was very close, and I had a very special childhood.

CHAPTER 3

The Gift of Grandparents

"Grandparents make the world ...
a little softer, a little kinder, a little warmer."

—*Unknown*

While growing up, my siblings and I often enjoyed many family gatherings with members of my dad's side of the family. My mom's family was scattered in several states, and we were unfortunately not able to see each other very often. But my Grandma and Grandpa Cooper always had a household of family home for the holidays, and we were there in the midst of the clamor. Their modest three-bedroom home often housed four or five families over Thanksgiving and Christmas, and there were wall-to-wall cousins, aunts, and uncles. Of course, it was much fun as a child because there were plenty of cousins to play with. On other occasions, we would visit my grandma and grandpa when no one else was around and we had their undivided attention.

The way our grandparents treated us felt different for my brother, sister, and me. Although my Grandma and Grandpa Cooper loved us, we were never really counted in as "theirs," because we were adopted. Although no one ever spoke these actual words, we understood them. I don't know if this mostly came from my grandpa or both of them. When my other cousins were around, my grandma and grandpa always held my cousins on their lap or in their arms. My brother, sister, and I never made it there.

I have memories of standing by my grandpa, and he would call me his "half-breed." As a little girl I never really knew what a "half- breed" was, but it felt uncomfortable. Later on, I can remember my mom and dad explaining the word in a positive light and saying the reason he used it was because of my (obvious) Indian heritage. Nonetheless, it left me with a sense of not belonging, and my heart was always broken when I heard that word. Although my grandpa probably didn't mean to hurt me, he did. My mom and dad's hearts must have been broken as well. I still loved my grandpa and was excited to see him, but things were always different. Although both my Grandma and Grandpa Cooper are gone now, I still look back on them with fond memories. They loved me; it was just in a different way than they did their other grandkids. But they did an awesome job of raising my dad. It was while my dad was living at home as a teenager that he surrendered his life to Jesus. For that rich heritage, I will forever be grateful.

My grandparents on my mom's side of the family were very loving and affectionate with toward my brother, sister and me. Some of the earliest memories I have of them standing in the yard in front of their house when we drove up, running to their open arms, and being smothered in hugs and kisses. There was no sense of being an outsider there. We fit right in. My fondest memories were of sleeping in my grandma's silky nighties on the couch while the scent of her gardenia hedges that surrounded their screened-in porch wafted inside the house. My Grandpa Harshberger loved gardening. While they lived in Florida, he grew the most beautiful roses I had ever seen, and his flower and vegetable gardens were spectacular. He always used to joke with us by saying the reason everything grew so big was because he used elephant manure. (Of course, it helped that my uncle was a veterinarian and was able to get my grandpa all the elephant manure he needed for gardening.) The flowers were big but I don't really know if the elephants had anything to do with it or not.

My grandparents also loved God with all their hearts. Tears would run down my grandma's cheeks as she shared stories of God's provision and faithfulness through her life. My grandma also told us about her "inventions" that always provided many laughs around the table. My grandpa never spoke much but when he did, he made it very clear that he loved me. I never tired of hearing those precious words, sitting on his lap or experiencing his enormous hugs.

Memories and Connections

"Consider the lilies, how they grow..."

Luke 6:27 (KJV)

One of my favorite memories while growing up happened when I was in grade school. Our family moved into a new parsonage that was a beautiful old Victorian-style home with many rooms, a large wraparound porch, and best of all ... a beautiful perennial flower garden along the entire south side of the house. Before that, I never really remember the delight of watching flowers grow and experiencing the wonder, beauty, and sweet fragrances as they blossomed. I was captivated by Lily-of-the-Valley flowers. These spring blossoms looked like soft little bells and their fragrance became my favorite. I decided that my favorite perfume would be anything that captured its essence. Little did I realize that Lily-of-the-Valley would hold a very special place in my heart in the future, but for a reason only God knew.

My dad was a great preacher. My life was molded under his precious teachings of God's Word. But he was also an avid vegetable gardener, and we had several small gardens. I have so many happy memories of watching him till the earth, carefully stretch string across the fragrant, black fertile soil with wooden stakes, and carefully plant seeds. My brother, sister, and I were often included in this fun event. Watching the seeds sprout and then grow into beautiful plants seemed like the best part of the summer. I have to admit that weeding the garden was not my forte, but my dad tenderly cared for it and seemed to have a knack for doing this. He would often reminisce about growing up on a farm and helping his dad with the chores. I think that gardening connected him with his past.

Although I loved watching the vegetables grow, my favorite was the flower garden. Dad never seemed to spend much time in the flowers, and my mom, who was raised in downtown Chicago, had no interest in gardening whatsoever. My dad told me the names of some of the flowers, and I remember sitting outside by them for hours and drinking in their beauty. It became my dream to someday plant flowers and be surrounded by them. I often wondered where this passion came from and why the vegetable garden didn't affect me like the perennial garden did. Now as I look back, I think that the flower garden somehow connected me to my past because I have since learned that my biological mother loved caring for her flowers as well.

My mom was a school teacher through and through. Some of my earliest memories of her were of her teaching in school and Sunday school, or leading Bible studies. I loved the way she engaged people and challenged them. Her ability to teach people of any age and help them discover new things always intrigued me. I determined at a very young age that I wanted to be just like her. Although I never became a school teacher, I have passionately been involved in the church, teaching at various levels. She taught me how to make learning fun for anyone.

My mom also loved people, and everyone loved her. But one of my best memories of my mom was listening to her sing. I have fond memories of her singing silly songs with us or humming in the kitchen as she worked. Her deep, rich voice was so soothing and sounded like velvet. In church, I would listen to her sing alto parts to the music during services, and I believe that sparked my appreciation of close harmony in acappella songs. Dad loved to play the guitar, piano, and organ. Our home was always filled with music. It was definitely a childhood made in heaven.

CHAPTER 5

Puzzle Pieces

*"Show me the right path, O LORD; point
out the road for me to follow."*

Psalm 25:4 (NLT)

I remember the day my desire to locate my biological family began to take shape. One of the biggest perks my dad got as a senior pastor was entertaining various missionaries as they visited our church. One missionary's visit rocked my world with curiosity. We were sitting around the table, enjoying a meal after the Sunday morning church service. The visitor wondered how I could be so much younger than my small older sister. After learning that my sister, brother and I were adopted, he said that he was sure I had Indian blood. He was a missionary at an American Indian Reservation out in South Dakota, and there was no question in his mind whatsoever as to my heritage. The wheels in my mind began to turn. Would that explain my nose and my jet-black hair?

I do remember growing up longing for physical familiarity. *What was I going to look like*, I wondered. My dad was a handsome man with auburn hair. He wore glasses, had a rather large nose, and was about six feet tall. His eyes were a beautiful blue that always sparkled. He was very strong, built very well, and had large hands. (My mom always said it was because he grew up on a farm and worked very hard.) My mom claimed to be about 5'6", and I always thought she must have been standing on a big phone book to get that high of a measurement. She wore glasses, had the most delicate turned-up nose, and very small, fragile-looking hands. Throughout all her life she battled with her weight, and she was on a constant diet to no avail. Her hair was black and curly, and she had the most beautiful piercing dark-brown eyes.

Even though I knew I was adopted, I longed to be like them. When I was in fifth grade it was suggested by a school teacher and determined by an optometrist that I needed glasses. That was probably one of the highlights of my childhood. Why? Because I was going to look like my mom and dad. The glasses covered my hazel eyes that didn't "fit in" and gave me a sense of belonging since they both wore glasses. My height I secretly attributed to my dad, and my black curly hair was from my mom. *But what about my nose?* My mom had the most beautiful nose there ever was. It was like a cute little ski jump, turned up and adorable. My dad had a definite Cooper nose, which just meant "big and wide." But, I was walking around through life with this nose that looked as though it was broken from several boxing matches. The sad thing: I never boxed a day in my life (although I did receive a few punches from my sister on several occasions).

I distinctly remember one day when I was playing softball (which I loved) in my backyard as a kid, I was pitching and caught a line drive directly on my nose. My glasses broke, and I'm sure my nose broke as well. But, that was my claim to fame and my proud explanation throughout my life as to my crazy nose. Every once in a while people would say to my parents, "Linda takes after her mom with her hair and her dad with her height." While growing up, those words were some of the best words an adopted kid could ever hear. We would never correct them by saying I was adopted. It became our family's secret reason to wink and chuckle afterward.

CHAPTER 6

The Flame of Curiosity

"Know Thyself"

—Inscription at the Delphi Oracle

When I graduated from high school, my parents told me my biological mother's full name. Unfortunately, that was all information they had about her. I knew I was born in Marion, Indiana, and the name of my biological mother's doctor was Dr. Boyer. They never hid this information from me, but I really wasn't that interested in more details, because I never really thought about my adoption when I was younger. After they told me my mother's full name, my mom and dad also said they would do everything they could to help me find her if I felt that desire. Now that I am older, I realize how unselfish their hearts were to reveal all that information and support me in my future endeavors to locate her. Mom and Dad knew that they and I shared a deep bond of love that grew even stronger as they supported me on this search.

My mind would frequently go back to that missionary who visited our home. His comments created a spark, and my curiosity grew about my heritage and my biological mother. But it wasn't until I went to college in Marion, Indiana (the town where I was born), that I thought more about my adoption.

One day, curiosity got the best of me, and I found a phone book. Believe it or not, there was a Dr. Boyer listed. I wrote down the number and quickly lost my nerve. An overwhelming sense of betraying my mom and dad came over me like a dark cloud. After visiting home one weekend, I mentioned to my mom and dad that I had found Dr. Boyer's phone number. They were excited for me and asked if I called her. I told them I hadn't, and I wasn't really sure if even I wanted to. They reassured me that they were all in favor of me finding my biological mother, but I buried the crazy idea again.

A few months later I came across the phone number I had written down, picked up the phone, and dialed Dr. Boyer. An immediate sense of panic came over me, and I began to shake. I remember thinking, *"What do I say? What if she answers?"* (You can probably tell that I am a bit compulsive and don't always think things through before acting. It has always been a downfall of mine.)

After several rings, an elderly lady answered. I asked her if she was Dr. Boyer, and she said she was. Then I introduced myself, explaining the information I had. I asked her if she knew Pauline Corby, my blood mother, and where she was living. Her answer caught me off guard. She told me I needed to let go of things and not stir up trouble. She then asked if I was having problems with my mom and dad, and I reassured her that we had a great relationship. Then she told me that Pauline had a great life and I needed to forget that I was adopted and leave things alone.

I remember hanging up from that conversation with my heart beating out of my chest. I had a hard time catching my breath, and I felt as if a ton of bricks had been dropped on me. How could I have been so foolish to call and even think about finding my biological mother? What was wrong with me?

I buried those feelings for several years and refused to open up those thoughts again.

CHAPTER 7

Nagging Questions

"But thou, O LORD, art a shield for me; my glory,
and the lifter up of mine head."

Psalm 3:3 *(KJV)*

Three years had passed since the call to Dr. Boyer, and after I had been married for a year, I found out I was pregnant. The flood of emotions about my biological mother began to consume my thoughts once again. I remember waking up every day with the joy of this baby inside me, and I couldn't imagine how my biological mother dealt with the fact that she was carrying a baby she knew she couldn't care for. My thoughts often turned to her, and I realized that I needed to continue the search. I wanted my baby to know his or her heritage from my side of the family and not just my husband's.

Every time when my husband and I filled out forms in the doctor's office, the medical staff would ask about our parents' health, and I always wrote across the top of the paper, "ADOPTED" and left everything else blank, mostly out of frustration. However, it would make me wonder about them. I would ask myself, *"Are they alive? Do they have any health problems? Are they struggling with any physical illnesses?*

I then determined that my children and their children would know some facts ... and there would be no more blank spaces on my medical forms.

CHAPTER 8

The Contact

"Your word is a lamp to guide my feet
and a light for my path."

Psalm 119:105 (NLT)

After leaving college, whenever I made a trip to Indiana from my home in Michigan, which was about once a year, I decided to visit the courthouse and go through huge record books. What began as a hobby type of search gathered momentum during my first pregnancy and I was determined to find some type of information. I checked the records for births, deaths, marriages, and the voter's registration archives, not to mention lots of microfilm. After three years of searching and gathering information, I hit the jackpot and found a current address for a man named Woodrow Horton, who, according to the records, married my biological mother after I was born.

I cannot tell you the surge of emotion that flooded over me. I was excited and yet scared to death that she wouldn't want anything to do with me. So, my plan was to knock on the door of their house and tell them who I was, leave them with a phone number, and give my mother time to consider if she would like to talk with me.

Driving up to that house was such a huge event. I was excited and nervous all at the same time. There was a tall, lanky man on the sidewalk leading up to the house who seemed to be setting up for some type of a yard sale. I walked up to him and asked him if he was Woodrow Horton, and he said yes.

Trying to choke back my excitement, I asked him if he was married to Pauline Corby and then he asked me why. I told him I was adopted, my birth mother was Pauline Corby, and that I was trying to locate her.

He was quiet for a bit and then asked me my birth date. I told him August 29, 1958, and he thought about it a bit longer. He then said the following quite matter-of-factly: I couldn't be her daughter because he was with her during that time and there was no way she had a baby. They were now divorced, and he would not share any more information.

I felt as though I had taken a punch to my gut, and I didn't know what to say. I somehow managed to thank him and walked back to the car ... and cried. I went from euphoria to devastation in a matter of three minutes. This trail to find my blood mother seemed impossible to follow.

That was the first and last time I saw Woodrow Horton (affectionately known as 'Woody'). I never knew I was speaking to my biological father and he never knew that he was talking to his first born child. My mother kept my birth and adoption a secret from everyone, including my father. He died several years later never knowing that I was his daughter.

A year later, I had another opportunity to go through more records in Indiana and found a phone number that matched up to my biological mother's new married name. Because I found this information at the last moment of my Indiana stay, I had no choice but to travel back to Michigan. That evening, once we arrived home, I had my husband call her ... because I knew I couldn't face another rejection.

The phone rang several times, and when someone answered, he asked for Pauline. It seemed to take forever before someone came to the phone. Then he asked, "Is this Pauline? Was your former name Pauline Corby?"

She answered with a reserved yes.

Did you have a daughter born August 29, 1958?"

It seemed as if an eternity of silence followed. Then she replied, "I had a daughter born on August 28, 1958 but let me think ... I suppose she could have actually been born on the 29th."

Then my husband said, "Well, I am married to her, and she would like to meet you someday if you would like. Let me give you our phone number, and you can think about it and call if you would like to meet her."

He waited for her to write down our number and then simply ended the conversation with a casual good-bye.

At last I thought. I was filled with a thousand questions. Was she excited about me finding her?

"No ... actually she was very quiet," my husband said.

"Did she ask any questions about me?"

"No."

"Do you think she'll call right back?"

"I don't know."

"What did her voice sound like?"

"I don't know."

That night my husband related the details of this conversation to me and I wasn't able to sleep a wink, imagining what might happen.

After that phone call I was on pins and needles for the next several days. Each time the phone rang I ran to answer it, anticipating my mother calling and wanting to meet me. But then I also had the dark fear of her wanting nothing to do with me. The words of Dr. Boyer haunted me.

Days passed with no call and then two weeks. By then I was sure that she wanted nothing to do with me, and I experienced such a deep, dark rejection. It is one thing to be given up once ... maybe it was a decision she didn't want to make and she really wanted to find me after all. But the thought of having the door slammed shut two times was almost unbearable.

CHAPTER 9

The Call

*Gracious words are a honeycomb, sweet to
the soul and healing to the bones."*

Proverbs 16:24 (NLT)

It was Easter Sunday, and our family had just enjoyed a big dinner. I was still sitting at the table when the phone rang. My husband answered it and then gave the phone to me. Not thinking anything about it, I said hello, and a soft Southern voice asked, "Deborah?"

I said, "No, this is Linda. Who are you calling?"

Then she said, "It's me. Pauline, your mother."

All the rehearsed words I planned to tell her if she ever called seemed to vanish from my mind. I was grabbing for something to say but nothing came out of my mouth. I felt totally vulnerable and raw. After catching my breath I told her that the name on my birth certificate was originally Deborah Sue Corby but my mom and dad changed my name to Linda Sue. I remember her telling me that Linda was a beautiful name too.

We both began to softly weep, and I tried to comfort her brokenness. She said that her pregnancy and my adoption was a deep, dark secret she had kept to herself all these years. I remember how I wanted to hear every word she spoke, but my heart was beating so loud that it was difficult to hear her tender Southern words.

She told me that she had waited these two weeks because she wanted to gather her family together for Easter dinner so she could tell everyone about me at the same time. Then she asked me not to hate her for giving me up for adoption.

I reassured her that I have always loved her, and I was thankful for the life she gave me. I also shared with her how my parents told me how brave and unselfish she was for making such a difficult decision. I told her that I had a wonderful life and how God had blessed me.

We exchanged addresses and phone numbers, and then she told me that there were some people who wanted to talk to me. I then learned that I had two brothers and two sisters. My mother later explained that a few years after my birth, Woody, my biological father, reentered her life, and they fell in love again and married. From this marriage she had two more children, Billy and Paula, who are my full-blooded siblings.

It was a day I'll never forget. Hearing everyone's voices on the phone began a healing process for both my mother and me. We had feared that that there would be hate, bitterness, and accusations when in fact it was just the opposite. Love and tenderness flowed between our hearts. Thankfully, we had both been wrong.

CHAPTER 10

Face-to-Face

"Like mother, like daughter."

—*Proverb*

A few months later we made arrangements, and the day finally arrived when we were able to meet each other face-to-face for the first time. I remember being filled with wild excitement and yet an equal amount of fear. *What if she doesn't like the way I look? Will she be ashamed of me?* I wondered.

As we made the plans over the phone to meet at one of her favorite restaurants in Indiana, I asked her, "How will you know who I am?"

She assuredly said, "Oh honey, I'll know who you are."

I didn't understand her confident reply, but I trusted her. As my husband and I drove fifteen minutes to the restaurant from our hotel room, I remember checking a mirror what seemed to be a million times. When we entered the restaurant, my heart was racing and it was hard to breathe.

Even before the hostess greeted us, I heard a gasp near the back of the dining room, and a white-haired lady stood up and began to cry with her arms outstretched toward me. I knew it was my mother. As she walked closer, it seemed as if I was looking into a mirror. My hair color was different (thanks to L'Oreal), but other than that, we were dead ringers for each other.

While attempting to eat, I remember trying not to stare at her face and hands, but we looked so much alike! It was an amazing feeling. In fact, my biological brothers and sisters have said that I look more like my mother than any of them. I've often wondered if God did this so there would be no question as to my "belonging" to my mother. It was obvious that she was my mother and I her daughter.

During that meal she told me she wanted me to forgive her for placing me for adoption. She said that she has felt guilty for this decision but had no other choice at the time. I reassured her that I loved her and that I was thankful for her decision to give me such a good life. I told her my parents were also thankful for her choice as well and God has blessed my life. After those words were spoken, we were able to talk about anything and everything.

As we began to walk out this new relationship, it became necessary to determine where to draw boundary lines. My mom and dad were my family and yet I just found my birth mother. I asked God for wisdom. There was an obvious connection between us and yet, when I was with her it felt talking to a distant aunt to whom I had blood ties but no history. Our visits consisted mainly of talking about family origins (which confirmed a rich Cherokee Indian ancestry), blood relatives, health, and God. I remember a lot of awkward pauses in the conversations.

Several years later, after going through a difficult divorce and then remarrying, I wanted my new husband, Gary, to meet my biological mother and her husband. I was thrilled to learn that my mother had arranged a special dinner at her house for us all to meet. Three out of my four siblings would join us as well as some aunts and uncles.

I distinctly remember being in the kitchen with my mother and sisters, Peggy and Paula, during that visit. Peggy grabbed my hand and looked at my thumb. She wanted to see if my thumb knuckle didn't bend. Indeed, my thumb was just like hers. If was sort of like my "proof of belonging." I guess I had never even thought about my thumb before, but I sure did about my nose, and yes, it belonged in *this* family! During that visit our four children were introduced to everyone as well. For my kids, I'm sure it went down in their diaries as another boring family gathering. But for me, it was the beginning of connecting.

From these various visits, we have decided that my oldest daughter, Calle', looks like my youngest sister when she was growing up. That was fun to discover. My son, Charles, reminds me of my brother, Rocky, and yet has similar traits of Billy, my youngest brother. My family has also determined that my youngest daughter, Chrissy, looks a lot like me and my mother. These discoveries connected many dots in my life that I had longed to see connected. Perhaps to men they seem foolish, but to a girl, it's a big deal!

CHAPTER 11

Raw Feelings

"" The LORD is close to the brokenhearted and
saves those who are crushed in spirit."

Psalm 34:18 (NIV)

An event that has stood out to me in my young-adult life was when my adoptive mom became very sick and her doctors determined that she should have a hysterectomy. My dad and I sat by her bedside in the hospital as she was recovering from the surgery. The doctor came by for his usual post-surgery checkup and shared with her some news that we were not expecting. He said that during the surgery he was able to determine why she was never able to conceive. She had scar tissue on her ovaries, fallopian tubes, and uterus from a botched emergency appendectomy she had when she was eleven years old.

This news caught us all by surprise, and my mom immediately began to cry. I didn't know what to do or what to say. I was sitting there listening to her grieve the pain of infertility that she had quietly carried all these years. To tell you the truth, I had never even considered her infertility and how that had affected her. It was a true testament of my selfishness because deep down in my own heart I was shamefully thankful that she didn't conceive and that Mom and Dad had adopted me.

I remember leaning over her bed and holding her while both our tears collected on her pillow. Her tears of deep sorrow mingled with my tears of shameful thankfulness. I couldn't help but think what might have happened to me if I hadn't been adopted into this wonderful family, and my heart burst with thanksgiving to my loving God. Later, as I look back on this event, I recognize that deep sorrow and deep joy are often part of the same journey, but God always works things out for good. A beautiful rainbow is often intermingled with dark clouds and rain.

God blessed me with three healthy pregnancies and births. So, during the birth of my son, I invited my mom into the labor room to help her experience the joy of the birthing process since she never experienced it herself. She was there the whole time, and she determined that she hadn't missed out on that much. I don't know if it was the twenty-four hours of labor, the intense pain, or the two hours of pushing, but she was then very thankful for never having experienced morning sickness, swollen ankles, and long labors.

I remember the doctor grinning and telling my mom as my son was born that it was tradition for the grandma to guess the birth weight, and if she guessed the right number, she could keep the baby. Luckily, she never guessed ten pounds. After pushing for so long, I thought that was a low number, but we were all very happy. Although I couldn't take away her pain of being barren, it brought my mom and me even closer as we experienced the miracle of birth together. The joy she experienced was priceless. It's a memory I'll carry with me forever.

CHAPTER 12

Common Bonds

"The LORD directs our steps so why try to understand everything along the way?"

Proverbs 20:24 (NLT)

The next few years were filled with visits back and forth between my biological mother and me. I'll never forget when she and I first visited each other's homes. We had two of the same Home Interiors decorations hanging on the wall, identical pictures, and the same color themes. Her house was filled with soft corral hues and candles just like mine. As I walked through my mother's home, I also saw my decorating taste displayed throughout each room. My adoptive mom never was a big fan of knickknacks or fancy little crystal vases, dishes, or candles, but I was and I never knew where I got it from until I visited my biological mother's home. One would think that these tendencies would be strictly environmental, but that wasn't the case with us.

Our visits were very sporadic. Neither Pauline nor I were good at writing. We called, but not often. Yet we knew we were there for each other and that alone filled a void in both our hearts. On my last longer visit to Tennessee, I spent a few days with Pauline before my family joined me. By that time she had been diagnosed with osteoporosis and bone cancer. She went from 5'9" to 5'2" and became very frail. I remember sitting with her and talking about life. She shared with me again her agonizing decision to place me for adoption and asked me to forgive her. I reassured her that I was thankful for her courageous and selfless decision to give me to my parents. How could I thank her enough for my wonderful mom and dad and family? I tried to explain how I could trace God's fingerprints on my life and how His plan was perfect. We laughed, cried, hugged each other, ate oatmeal together for breakfast, watched *Wheel of Fortune* together in the evenings, and I then gave her a Bible I purchased especially for her. I shared with her the difference that God had made in my life.

As she listened, tears welled up in her eyes, and she told me that her most precious possession was her relationship with God. She said if it wasn't for His grace and His mercy, she would not have been able to survive all she had been through. She was surprised to receive my first letter after our first phone conversation, twenty-two years earlier, explaining how I had surrendered my life to God and how my heart was filled with love for her. She said it released her from years of guilt, anger, and bitterness. Since then, she had asked God to be her Savior, and she committed her future to Him.

We talked about heaven and how special it was going to be. But still, I believe, we both had unanswered questions in our hearts as to why this time of suffering was allowed in our lives.

CHAPTER 13

Lily of the Valley

"For where your treasure is, there your heart will be also."

—Luke 12:34 (NIV)

The fall of 2005 a missionary conference was held in our church. My husband and I attended and especially enjoyed listening to a couple who were the directors of Lily of the Valley (Lirio de los Valles) orphanage in Chihuahua, Mexico. In fact, their faith and testimony really challenged our hearts.

On the way home from church, I mentioned that I would someday like to visit an orphanage, but my husband did not respond. Later that evening our friends asked us to visit their home and said that directors of the orphanage would be there as well. We were tired and debated whether or not we should go, but we went. Little did we realize that this visit would drastically change our lives.

As we arrived at our friend's home, we gathered around the dining room table and became enthralled by the conversation. Ed and Rosa Salo told us about their orphanage and the one hundred-plus children who lived there. We listened to many stories of faith. For example, when they had no food, the children prayed and food arrived. They also told us of the challenges of raising so many children. I remember asking them if it was difficult finding enough pillows for all the kids to sleep at night. Their reply was simple: The children didn't have pillows. They had a bed and a blanket only.

I asked if it seemed impossible to keep up with the children's need for socks and underwear, since that was always a challenge while raising my children. Rosa said they barely had enough.

I don't really remember the rest of the conversation after that because my mind was spinning. I felt compelled to get pillows, socks, and underwear to those kids.

Before leaving, Ed and Rosa asked us to come and visit them. I told them I'd love to, but I had no idea if my husband would be interested. They had mentioned that they had vehicles that desperately needed repairs, so I held on to that, praying that my husband's heart would be challenged as well since he is a professional mechanic. On the way home that evening I told him that I'd love to take our family down to the orphanage for Christmas. He said that would never happen, so I began to pray in faith, like the orphans I just heard about had done.

Two weeks later my husband asked me how I thought we could ever afford to fly our family to Mexico. I didn't have any idea how it would work, but I felt compelled more than ever to go.

By November, we made reservations for our young-adult children to fly with us. To tell you the truth, I was more excited for them to go than for myself. They were all at pivotal points in their lives, and they had their whole futures in front of them. I was hoping that God might call them to work with orphans someday.

Our church was one hundred percent behind us, and another family from our church decided to join our adventure. So on Christmas Day 2005, we flew down to Mexico with suitcases filled with socks, underwear, pillowcases, and enough money to purchase 150 pillows and any other needed items. We flew in at night, and a busload of orphans greeted us at the airport. That began our love relationship.

I remember hearing earlier that the children had lice and ringworm. My intention was to carefully hold the children on the edge of my knees and keep them at arm's length to protect my health. That changed when the first child crawled onto my lap. They looked up at me with their big brown eyes, and all my preconceived notions and plans went out the window. I held these children closely and kissed them as though there was no tomorrow. We had an instant camaraderie. We had tasted each other's sorrow, and we understood the pain of rejection and abandonment. The children and I immediately connected, and my heart was broken for them.

I began asking Ed and Rosa questions about the children, wondering how many of them had been adopted. They told me only one had. I couldn't believe it. That night I couldn't sleep, and I felt as though I needed to help make a difference. During the next few days, I asked the directors of the orphanage what was necessary to make adoptions happen, and they said it took hours of research, lots of paperwork, and many trips to the government offices for the children to have "orphan status," which they needed to have to be adopted.

The week passed quickly, and it was soon time to go. As we flew home, my heart was broken. I cried the whole way. Gary was quiet too, but our kids seemed rather relieved to return to "civilization." When we drove up to our house, I felt foolish and guilty to own such a beautiful home when our new friends lived in such extreme poverty. Our first night home I felt numb. The sweet faces of the children kept on popping into my thoughts. My ability to function seemed warped. As my husband and I opened up our auto repair shop the next morning, our bodies were there, but our hearts were not.

Out of the blue, I said to my husband that I thought we should move down to Mexico and work at the orphanage. I waited for his negative response. Instead he told me that maybe we should write them and ask if they thought they could use someone like us. I couldn't believe it. I remember grabbing my computer and typing up a letter and printing it. Gary read it and signed it. Then we talked about how long it would take for the letter to arrive in Mexico through snail mail. Our hearts were so connected to Mexico that we couldn't bear the long wait of one to three months. Finally, Gary suggested that I just call them.

Before he could finish the words, I was dialing their number. Rosa answered the phone and was surprised to hear from us. I told her what we were thinking about, and her response was, "Linda, this morning when we gathered for prayer, we asked the Lord to send someone just like you and Gary to help us."

Well, that sealed it in our minds. Somehow, someday, we would end up at the orphanage to make a difference in the lives of the children there. Our hopes and dreams for our children to feel the urgency to work at an orphanage seemed to have backfired, and our hearts were the ones that could think of nothing else.

CHAPTER 14

Connecting Dots

"Father to the fatherless ... God places the lonely in families ... and gives them joy."

—Psalm 68:5-6 (NLT)

It has been several years now since our first visit to Mexico, and we have made many trips back and forth to the orphanage. God has allowed me to work on the orphan status for many children and discover children who are eligible for adoption. Presently eleven children from the orphanage have been adopted by families in our church. There are other children with orphan status waiting on adoption as well. Families from all over the United States have filed to adopt many of them. I can't begin to tell you how fulfilling this is.

While growing up insecurity ran wild. I never understood why I was adopted. Questions plagued me. *"What was wrong with me? Why was I given up for adoption? If my mother already had two other children, why would she want to give me up? I thought every baby was beautiful. Was I not?"*

These thoughts often invaded my mind, but I learned to bury them for lack of answers. As I grew older, I realized how God has a master plan and He causes everything to work out for good. Still, I couldn't connect the dots. It wasn't until I began working on the children's paperwork in Mexico that I would be able to perhaps catch a glimpse of God's plan. If I hadn't been adopted into such a great family and experienced the success of a wonderful adoption, I wouldn't have desired the same for the children at the orphanage. In fact, I am sure I wouldn't have even thought about it.

I don't believe for one second that it is God's plan for children to be abandoned or hurt, but because of sin, it unfortunately happens. However, God does allow for children to be placed in loving homes, through adoption, and they can experience the joy of a family (Psalm 68:5).

On previous visits to the orphanage, my heart would always break when many of the children would ask me if I could find a family for them ("beg" would be a more accurate description). I told them that God orchestrated the adoptions, not me, and they needed to ask Him for a forever family. I have always felt so empty and sad because there are only a few children who will be able to experience adoption by a family from the United States. It wasn't until my recent visit to Mexico that God revealed more truths to me about adoption. I realized that my greatest adoption story was not my adoption by my mom and dad, but my adoption by my heavenly Father. He is the one who truly filled the void in my life. He is the one who rescued me from a wretched life of despair and gave me hope, joy, and a future. God used my mom and dad to provide me with an earthly home filled with fun and laughter. But God has prepared for me an eternal home that will surpass all my hopes and dreams. My heavenly Father has promised that He will never leave me or abandon me and that I can live with Him forever!

During my latest visit to the orphanage, the children asked me several questions as they usually do. One child asked me, "Do you remember feeling sad and lonely before you were adopted." Of course my answer was no since I was adopted at birth. But then another child asked me if I felt sad and lonely before I was a Christian. Even though I was only four or five years of age when I became a Christian, I do remember the horrible guilt of my sin and the heaviness in my heart. It was not until I asked, as a little girl, for Jesus to wash away my sin that I truly experienced peace and joy. That is the adoption that filled me with hope and put the song in my heart.

I realized at that point that I had great news for all the children! The director of the orphanage asked me to prepare a message to share with them on Easter Sunday morning since we were unable to make it to church in the nearby town. I knew what message I wanted to share: my favorite adoption.

"Boys and girls," I excitedly announced. "I am happy to tell you this morning that every one of you has the opportunity to be adopted."

They were shocked and immediately the room was filled with excitement.

"My heavenly Father wants to adopt every one of you into His family." I continued to explain that earthly adoptions are not perfect. That the children have big hopes and dreams and the adoptive family has big hopes and dreams, but not all of these dreams come true, and there are times of disappointment and heartache because of sin that has entered the world.

"But when you are adopted into God's family, He will never disappoint you," I continued. "He will always be with you, and He will never abandon you."

Then I told them about their new home that is being prepared for them in heaven. "It is being built by the greatest carpenter in the world," I said. "In fact, the creator of the world is working on a perfect home just for you! The best part is that it will last *forever* and no one can take it away."

Later that week, I talked to several children about surrendering their lives to God and the opportunity to be adopted into God's family. Twenty-four of the children and teens surrendered their lives to Jesus and trusted Him for their hope and future.

At this time, God again reminded me of my greatest treasure: my "second" adoption. My earthly mother and parents provided me with a good childhood, a great home, and nurturing, for which I will be eternally thankful. But my greatest treasure is the adoption by my heavenly Father. He paid the highest price for me by sending His only Son to die on a cross just for my ransom. My heavenly Father loves me unconditionally and tenderly cares for me throughout each day. I am now never alone. Someday I will leave this earth and join Him in heaven where I will be with Him forever. The greatest part is that I will be with all my family: My heavenly Father, my mother, and my mom and dad. I am not home yet, but I am looking forward to that great reunion.

Adoptions are very special because a child is cherished enough by the birthmother to be granted the gift of life, given away for the hope of a better life, chosen by a family, and loved beyond measure. They become a permanent heir and member of a family unit who brings great joy. But the greatest adoption one can experience is the adoption into the family of God.

Once I was able to see the children adopted into loving homes, my life became filled with purpose and motivation. But until they are adopted into God's family, they won't experience true peace and the promise of a great future. It doesn't matter if only one or eleven children from the orphanage are adopted or if there will be a hundred children adopted from Mexico to the United States. My main focus now is praying that they will all surrender their lives to God and become a part of His family, no matter where they live.

CHAPTER 15

Our Precious Bond

"The faithful love of the LORD never ends! His mercies never cease. Great is his faithfulness; his mercies begin afresh every morning. I say to myself, "The LORD is my inheritance; therefore, I will hope in him."

Lamentations 3:22-24 (NLT)

The few visits I had with my biological mother seemed to go by much too quickly, and there were always the dreaded "good-byes." I would cry for the first hour we were separated on the drive home, and she shared with me that she did the same. It wasn't until recently that I realized this connection: my mom and dad have always told me that when they first got me, I was an "eight-ounce formula baby" from day one. (In fact, that was my number-one baby "claim-to-fame" story.) As a newborn, my parents said I cried and so they fed me. After four ounces of formula, I kept crying, so they gave me four more to drink. I've heard the story for years, and now I wonder about the reason for my tears. During that first month, was I crying from hunger or crying from a broken heart? Could it be that my hunger was for a familiar voice and I was afraid? Was I crying out for my mother, that familiar voice, the embrace I never received? (I now know she was crying for me.) Was I grieving a separation that I could not understand?

I now believe there was a familiarity of tears in being separated from my mother at birth and in her death. There were tears and deep pain of separation at my mother's graveside, but also in my first few days of my life. I didn't need more formula as an infant; I was grieving the loss of my mother, a very painful good-bye.

I saw my mother one last time as my husband and I were traveling down to Mexico. We met her for dinner, and I shared with her once again how her decision to place me in a loving Christian home has not only impacted my life but the lives of many other families. Children who were once lonely orphans are now experiencing the joy of a family because of her actions. Her one selfless decision has rippled into beautiful stories of love and hope. Although our visit was short, I still remember the tender love we shared. The separation once again brought tears.

CHAPTER 16

Difficult News

"For everything there is a season, a time for every activity under heaven. A time to be born and a time to die."

Ecclesiastes 3:1-2a (NLT)

I will never forget the phone call I received at the age of fifty-two from my biological brother, Rocky. It came on a beautiful Indian summer day in September while I was enjoying a Sunday afternoon drive with my husband. I was hoping for a phone call from him since he knew I had been trying to call my mother for the past couple of months and had not been able to talk with her. During the past two years, I had been struggling with my health, and I was not able to see Pauline as I had planned. It seemed whenever I tried to reach her in Tennessee, she was visiting Paula or Rocky in Florida, and we had only three successful phone calls during that time. During the last call I had from my mother, she told me she would love to hold me one last time. She cried and begged me to visit her, so I made it my goal to spend some time with her. However, I was battling a bad kidney infection and was unable to travel, so it never worked out. When I tried to call her, there was no answer. Later, I learned that her health was declining rapidly, and she was living in Florida with my brother and sister. They had their hands full caring for her, and apparently she was not able to return my calls. I did send her a birthday card in August and sent my love, but that was the last of our communication on this earth.

During that phone call, Rocky told me she had died in my sister's home. She was happy, watching TV with her grandchildren and then laid down for a nap. She was lovingly tucked into bed by her granddaughter, and then she woke up in heaven. I was so thankful Rocky called me, and later in the week I learned about the funeral arrangements in Tennessee. The funeral wouldn't be for two weeks since her body had to be transported from Florida to Tennessee, and there were a lot of arrangements that had to be made.

When I hung up, I was numb. I wanted to see her one last time, but now it was too late. Tears overwhelmed me, and I ached for her. Feelings of abandonment began to flood my soul until my husband gently reminded me that it wasn't her choice to leave me this time. In fact, she was a fighter. She had courageously battled bone cancer for many years, and she was not a quitter. Jesus had just called her home.

CHAPTER 17

Good-Bye ... Hello

Be merciful to me, Lord, for I am in distress; my eyes grow weak with sorrow, my soul and body with grief."

Psalm 31:9 (NIV)

During the next two weeks I felt crippled. My body and my heart were somehow detached, and it was difficult to function. I knew I wanted to attend my mother's funeral, but I had no idea if anyone would want me there. After all, I was not "legally" her daughter, but my mother and I knew in our hearts that we were mother and daughter, no questions asked. The only problem was that she would not be able to welcome me and make everything all right. I finally determined to go to the funeral because she was my mother and I loved her. If there was anything I could do to make things easier for my siblings, such as run errands, that was what I wanted to do.

I remember the long fourteen-hour drive to the funeral in Tennessee with my husband. With each mile marker that clicked by, memories would flash before my eyes: the first time we met, our first embrace, her witty sense of humor, the look on her face when she met my children, and her plea for one last embrace. Tears marked our trail to Tennessee as well as apprehension.

We finally arrived at our hotel, and it was a very welcoming place to land. Apparently it was Alumni Weekend for Tusculum College, so most of the other hotels were booked up. We stayed at the General Morgan Inn, located in downtown Greeneville, Tennessee, a beautiful historical landmark of the South. Built in the late 1800s, it was completely restored to its original grandeur. The lobby had gorgeous lead-crystal chandeliers, and everything was exquisitely elegant. Our room had twelve-foot ceilings, a fireplace, and the most amazingly comfortable bed. We quickly cleaned up from a long trip and were dressing for the viewing when my phone rang. It was Rocky, my brother. He wanted to make sure we arrived safely and that we knew the viewing started at six. Hearing his voice calmed my nerves, and I felt reassured that I had made the right decision to go.

When we arrived at the funeral home, the parking lot was full, so we parked in the back corner. My knees were knocking, and I was about to shake right out of my shoes. My prince grabbed my arm and led me into the funeral parlor. I remember stopping just inside the doorway and seeing a room full of strangers. I suddenly thought, *Linda, if this isn't the dumbest thing you have done. No one knows you, so what are you going to do now?*

After what seemed like ten minutes (my husband said it was only about one, though), Paula, my youngest sister, came up to me and gave me a big hug. I hadn't seen her in about six years, but she still looked the same—very beautiful. Then my oldest sister, Peggy, gave me a big hug, followed by Billy, my youngest brother. I was very excited and yet apprehensive to meet my oldest brother, Rocky, for the first time. Although I had talked to him over the phone, I had never met him in person. I didn't know what their reaction might be, but when I was introduced to Rocky, he gave me a big old hug and I melted. Now, there are differences in hugs. There are hugs and then there are *hugs*. Well, I received *hugs* from all of them, and I can't begin to explain how comforting they were. My sister Paula introduced me again to her two beautiful daughters and her son whom I hadn't seen for six years as well. Then my oldest sister introduced me to her granddaughter, whom I had never met.

There are no words for a moment like that. I remember crying and shaking and reminding myself to breathe. Shortly after that I was introduced by Paula to aunts and uncles, some whom I'd never met. Then I was reacquainted with some relatives I had met briefly four years earlier. Before we left the viewing that evening, I asked my brothers and sisters what time the funeral was, just to make sure I had it right. They told me that the funeral was at 11:00 a.m. but family was supposed to be there at ten thirty. Then I asked them what time they would like for me to arrive. They looked at me quite matter-of-factly and said 10:30.

Oh my goodness ... *Did this mean I was really part of the family?* Words can't describe the jubilant elation, matched with pure joy, that flowed through me. I went from feeling unworthy to even attend this viewing to being lavished with love and acceptance. I wish there were words to describe how exhilarating that was.

As Gary and I walked out to our car, I had to go slowly because my legs could barely hold me up. It wasn't from standing up for the past two hours; it was from trembling with excitement and the total wonder of being accepted into this family. I was bawling for joy; the tears were never ending. I entered the funeral home as an outsider and left as a member of a loving family that deeply cared about me. I remember crying out, *"Jesus, I don't deserve this."* Once again, I was in awe of my big God.

As we walked into our hotel that night, there was a sweet refrain of music flowing through the air from the second-floor terrace party. Down the hall there was an exquisite ball and reception taking place. Everyone was dressed up in elegant attire, and the air was filled with magical excitement. I felt like Cinderella. I wept as my prince held me tight, and we talked about our gracious God, one who would pour out such blessings.

I don't think I slept a wink that night. My thoughts would return to my mother and the undeserved love of two brothers and two sisters and my new aunts and uncles. My mind was whirling. I was really part of a big family I never realized I had. Although my heart ached from the finality of never seeing Pauline on this earth, I was overcome with joy at the thought of seeing her once again in heaven. There would be no more good-byes. Then I thought about my brothers and sisters again, and my heart felt like it would burst with thanksgiving to God.

Morning finally arrived, bright and sunny. Gary and I were up early enough to have a leisurely time dressing and enjoying the Chocolate Café, which served a wonderful chocolate chai. My Bible was in the car, so I was elated to find a Gideon's Bible in a drawer in the dresser near my bed. I opened it and read the wonderful words of Jeremiah 29:11 that opened up right in front of me. "For I know the plans I have for you, says the Lord. They are plans for good and not for disaster, to give you a future and a hope."(NLT) Then I flipped through the pages to Proverbs 3:5–6. "Trust in the Lord with all your heart, lean not on your own understanding. In all your ways acknowledge Him and He will make your path straight." (NIV) Before closing the Bible the pages fell open to Isaiah 55:8–9. "My thoughts are nothing like your thoughts,' says the Lord. 'And my ways are far beyond anything you could imagine. For just as the heavens are higher than the earth, so my ways are higher than your ways and my thoughts higher than your thoughts." (NLT)

I was in awe of a God who orchestrated such a beautiful plan for my life.

Gary and I drove to the funeral home and met up with my family. I could tell by the tearstained faces of my siblings that they had not slept much the night before, either. I remember feeling almost guilty because my night had included rejoicing along with the sorrow and tears. Yes, I was grieving the loss of my mother, but I was also elated to receive the loving embrace of my siblings.

As the funeral director wheeled the casket out of the viewing room, he asked for the children of Pauline to follow behind, and her brothers and sisters were to follow after that. I stood off to the side because I still didn't think of myself as one of the "official" children yet. When my brothers and sisters saw I wasn't there, they said, "Come on, Sis." I bowed my head and walked toward them with my husband. Tears streamed down my face. *They asked me to sit with them and called me "Sis."* I was not prepared for that.

The word *sis* kept ringing through my head. *Sis.* I liked that word. No, I *loved* the sound of that word coming from them.

We walked into the chapel, and the service began with some precious songs that my sister, Paula's, daughters had arranged on a CD. These songs were very meaningful to the girls, my sisters and brothers, and my mother, a vivid reminder of the fun times they shared. I remember sitting there as my brothers and sisters quietly mouthed the words to songs that were sadly unfamiliar to me. I felt a twinge of jealousy that they were able to enjoy these songs together with my mother and the closeness they must have felt.

Once the songs finished, the girls shared with the congregation some heartfelt words about their precious relationship with their "nana." The minister then stood and began to read the obituary.

I snuggled next to my husband, and the obituary began with the dates of her birth and death. Then it said she was survived by her children. I lovingly looked at each one of them as the minister read their names. And then I heard, "and Linda Beggs." *My name! It was my name! Was there some kind of mistake? No, I heard my name! I was listed as her daughter.* Uncontrollable sobs began flowing out of me. I was not prepared to hear my name listed as her daughter, as an official part of the family. For the next few minutes I tried to gain control of this overwhelming feeling. The tears would not stop, and I was shaking uncontrollably. It was then that I caught a glimpse of what it might be like in heaven. Someday I will stand before my Savior, and my name will be called, listed as His child in the Lamb's Book of Life. I know that I am a child of God, but I think when I hear my name officially read, I will weep and be lost in the wonder of belonging to my King.

I cannot tell you much of the sermon the pastor shared, because the thrill of being listed as a daughter took me several minutes to absorb. Did I feel worthy? No. But I was listed nonetheless. I do remember the pastor talking about storms in life and how Jesus calms them. I wanted to add that He not only calms the storms, but He allows them for His glory. When we make it through the storm, we cherish the calm and we bask in its serenity.

I couldn't help but think how nonchalantly my siblings listened to their names being read and how hearing my name completely overwhelmed me. In fact, to this day, I will admit that this moment was definitely one of the highpoints of my life. I am still trying to understand why. I think this is the reason: I love my mom and dad and I love my adoptive family. I had such a great life, and I thought it was complete. But hearing my name read in my mother's obituary brought me back full circle. I was given up for a time and then reclaimed. My life counted. I mattered. I was included.

After the funeral Gary and I joined the funeral procession to the graveyard, which was several miles away. I remember sitting in our car and trying to tell my husband how it felt to hear my name listed as her daughter. He knew the depth of this because of my tears, but I don't know if there are words to explain its breadth. I couldn't help but say, "He read my name. He read my name. I am listed as a daughter."

When we arrived at the cemetery, it was breathtakingly beautiful. It overlooked the Great Smokey Mountains in their entire splendor. There was a blue canopy over two small rows of chairs and in front of these was the casket that held my dear mother. I stood on the outside the canopy looking in and my brother, Billy, led me up to the front row. My tears began to flow again by this inclusion. The gravesite was on a hillside, so we didn't dare sit back in our chairs for fear of tipping back. I sat there next to my precious sisters and aunts as we listened to the committal service. To be honest, I don't recall much of the minister's words except hearing about my mother's final destination: heaven. There was a prayer, and the service was over. My brothers made sure I had a flower from the casket spray to keep, and I gratefully held on to it.

It was then that I felt I needed to say good-bye to my mother, so I walked over to the casket and laid my hands on it. The wellspring of tears that flooded over me caught me by surprise. I wept and I didn't want to leave. Sobs overtook me, and I grieved a loss I felt to my innermost being. It was so deep and moving, like nothing I've ever experienced before and yet vaguely and hauntingly familiar.

Perhaps I was mourning the absence of my mother who couldn't care for me. Maybe I was grieving what could have been. But I honestly believe that I cried those same gut-wrenching tears one other time in my life as a newborn when my mother and I were separated by an unknown future. This time, however, it was different because I knew our future. I will see her again in heaven. I just don't know when.

After the funeral, Gary and I were invited to my mother's house by my sisters and brothers. As we arrived, I dreaded the thought of walking into her house and not feeling her loving embrace and hearing her sweet, welcoming Southern voice. I thought it would be unbearable, but as soon as we entered her house, my sister Paula and my brother Rocky welcomed us and made us feel right at home. Soon afterward the house was filled to capacity with aunts, uncles, cousins, and their children. Stories of years gone by filled the afternoon with much love and laughter. Aunts and uncles introduced themselves to me, and I again was overwhelmed by the outpouring of love.

As we were sitting around the table, my brother Billy told me something that I will treasure the rest of my life. He said our mother's birthday was August 20, and she always was sad and cried for about two weeks after it. No one could ever figure out why until that Easter Sunday when they learned about my birth on August 29. They realized then that she was grieving my absence in her life. She always wondered what became of me and if I was all right. Likewise, I also spent every birthday wondering if she ever thought about me. Now I know she did. My brother's words brought healing.

One particular uncle I had just met at the funeral home felt bad because he had just learned about me three years ago, and he didn't want to "lose" me again. I reassured him that we would keep in contact. Another aunt pulled me aside and shared with me a precious story about my mother. She said that she remembered how my mother became very bitter against God after I was adopted. Although Pauline couldn't care for me, she always felt like a failure for this decision. My aunt said that things changed drastically in Pauline's life after I found her. Oh how I remember that joyous time during one of our visits when my mother told me about giving her life to Jesus! Perhaps my re-entry into her life gave her the desire to seek healing and forgiveness through God. If that is true, my journey to find her also served an eternal purpose.

CHAPTER 18

My Big Brother

"Christ ... is your example, and you must follow in His steps."
—1 Peter 3:21 (NLT)

All through my life I was told by my adoptive parents that I have an older brother as well as a sister. I would look at families with an older brother and think, "Boy, I wish I knew mine!" In my Pollyanna-ish mind-set, I imagined my older brother would be available 24/7 for me, his little sister. He would protect me, watch out for me, and help guide me through life. I could always trust him and depend on him.

The other day while I was driving in my car, I was crying out to God. I was feeling blue because the big brother I have found (my biological big brother) was not the big brother I had longed for. (Actually, no one on this earth could have filled the role of all I had dreamed him to be.)

After pouring out my heart to the Lord, He gently shared with me this thought: "Linda, you know that Jesus is my Son, right?"

"Yes, Father, I know that!" The reminder made me feel as though He were talking to a child.

Then He said, "Linda, I have adopted you, and you are my daughter."

"Yes, Father, I know!" Still, I felt as though I was sitting through a simple Sunday school lesson I had learned many years ago.

The next words He spoke to me rocked my world. "Linda, you have the big brother you have always longed for. His name is Jesus." Tears began to flow and I was overwhelmed by this simple revelation. "Let Him be your hero."

That simple truth took my breath away. I was overwhelmed with joy and thankfulness. Jesus is not only my Savior but my big brother to guide me through life. That revelation has brought me such joy. My true identity is in God's family.

I also remember that throughout my life I have longed for a resemblance to a family member. Since I have been dwelling more on my "second adoption" by God, I have been reminded that my real goal is to resemble Jesus Christ (my real big brother). My search is over! I have someone to pattern my life by and someone to strive to be like. Now I am longing to hear the words, "Her actions remind me of Jesus." An even better thought is for my heavenly Father to think that I resemble His Son. That is the ultimate family connection that my heart has yearned for since birth!

CHAPTER 19

Forgiveness

"To forgive is to set a prisoner free and discover the prisoner was you."

—Unknown

After my mother's funeral, I listened to many Bible teachings, and they all seemed to be on forgiveness. I heard how we need to forgive because we have been forgiven. I honestly wondered why these lessons were coming across my path because I didn't feel as though I was harboring unforgiveness at all. It seemed like wasted time to me until I realized God was leading me down a pathway of healing and I needed to listen closely.

Throughout my life, I have been presented with the blessings of my adoption. My mother loved me so much that she wanted a better life for me than she could provide. Even though it broke her heart, she gave me to a loving couple who were praying for a baby. I've rehearsed these words throughout my entire lifetime and I have celebrated this decision over and over. But it wasn't until listening to these lessons on forgiveness that the Holy Spirit helped me realize that I need to forgive my biological mother.

You see, deep down inside my heart was a girl who wondered what was wrong with her. I knew the circumstances, I understood the loving sacrifice my biological mother made, but still ... I had been abandoned. My mother "kept" four children, and I was the one given away. I was driving up to the pregnancy center where I volunteer when I came to this realization. All those secret, dark years of feeling like a failure overwhelmed me, and I realized that I needed to release her as well as myself by uttering words of forgiveness. Tears flowed freely down my cheeks as I said, "Pauline, I forgive you. I forgive you."

I can't begin to explain the freedom I experienced, as if a huge weight had been pulled away from my heart. Joy has taken residence where unspoken dark questions had once resided. My heart is light. I am free.

CHAPTER 20

Blood Is Thicker than Water

"But if we walk in the light, God himself being the light, we also experience a shared life with one another, as the sacrificed blood of Jesus, God's Son, purges all our sin."

—1 John 1:7 (NASB)

"So you have not received a spirit that makes you fearful slaves. Instead, you received God's Spirit when he adopted you as his own children. Now we call him, "Abba, Father."

—Romans 8:15 (NLT)

"Blood is thicker than water." I heard this phrase often while growing up and I never know what to do with it. Each time I heard it, I was quietly reminded of the fact that I had no "blood" ties to my family, and it was very unsettling the older I got. Often I wondered if I would somehow feel closer to my mom and dad if their blood flowed through my veins, even though I couldn't imagine a closer relationship than I shared with them.

Did that saying mean we weren't truly connected? I sadly wondered this for many years until my favorite adoption revelation took place. I realized that I did have a blood connection to my family. It's the blood of Jesus Christ. The blood He shed on the cross over two thousand years ago connected me not only to Him, but to other believers, including my mom, dad, and mother. That is the blood that is thicker than water.

I have four biological siblings who are very special to me. A biological/bloodline connection is definitely there. But our conversations at this point are quite shallow and practically nonexistent since we don't have much history to share. When I was adopted by my mom and dad, I received two other siblings, and they are a very important part of my life. We enjoy talking about things that happened in our childhood, and we love to compare notes on fun memories.

However, my second adoption into God's family has given me brothers and sisters in Christ who are too numerous to count. Our connection? The same precious blood of Jesus Christ. His blood paid the adoption fee for me, and I am a member of a great family that I have a sweet fellowship with. The greatest thing is that I am meeting new members of my family wherever I go. It extends around the globe, and when we get together to talk, we share a bond that is deeper than any I know on this earth. Our favorite thing to talk about? Our heavenly Father.

CHAPTER 21

Conviction

"'For I know the plans I have for you,'" says the LORD. 'They are plans for good and not for disaster, to give you a future and a hope.'"
—Jeremiah 29:11 (NLT)

"And we know that in all things God works for the good of those who love him, who have been called according to his purpose."
—Romans 8:28 (NIV)

Conclusion

If you would ask me if adoptions are good, I would quickly say yes. Are they easy? No. Through the years, I have had the privilege of walking alongside single girls giving up their babies for adoption. Only one was able to go through the adoption process, and the other girls kept their babies.

The girl who placed her baby with another family struggled with many tears and months of heartache. Placing her baby for adoption was heart-wrenching, even though the birth mom knew she was making a good decision for both her and the baby. Most adoption agencies have amazing counselors who guide the birth moms through the entire process and continue to help even after the baby is born.

My heart bled right alongside this brave girl because I was somehow able to taste the tears of my biological mother through her heartache. I believe God gave me that experience so I would be able to appreciate the sacrificial gift of life that my mother gave me. God has also given me the opportunity to walk alongside couples praying for a baby, and I watched the Lord give them their hearts' desire. The sheer joy they experienced as they held their "miracle" brought such joy to me. I was able to catch a glimpse of the excitement my mom and dad felt as they held me for the very first time.

Adoption agencies do a tremendous job preparing birth mothers and couples who are hoping to adopt. But there are risks involved. Birth moms can change their minds; countries who have had many successful adoptions to the United States can suddenly close all foreign adoptions down; adoption fees have sky rocketed; the adopted children may be older and unwilling to open up their hearts to their new parents; and the list goes on.

Adoption is hard. You will experience many sleepless nights, cry many tears, and be frustrated to the point of despair. But God is faithful. If He is in the adoption process, it will be worth it. God doesn't promise life will be easy. He just promises to be faithful. If God is calling you to follow His great example to adopt, do it. Then put on your seat belt and get ready for the ride of your life.

Both of my adoptions have caused me to be a greater mom, grandma, wife, and tia (aunt) to the orphans in Mexico. I cherish ordinary moments and often realize that I have been given "second chances" through my first and second adoption.

Would I have written a plan like this for my life? Probably not. Would I rewrite my story if I could? No. When I look back on my life, I wouldn't trade this path for anything. I have been given so much love from a remarkable mother, mom, and dad. But my greatest adoption story is that of my heavenly Father. He has filled my life with joy, peace, and hope. God orchestrated a beautiful song out of heartache and exchanged sorrow for joy. In fact, He seems to specialize in that—creating beauty from ashes.

Although I have said my final good-bye to my biological mother, I have said hello to two new brothers, two new sisters, precious cousins and aunts and uncles with whom I hope to know better through the years. I have both lost and gained so much, which seems to be the theme throughout life. My mother is now in heaven, and I will see her again someday. It will be a precious reunion with no more good-byes. Until then I am enjoying the privilege of being called "Sis" by Peggy, Rocky, Billy, Paula, and my precious newly discovered cousin, Jean.

I am anxious to share with my sisters and brothers my favorite adoption story where Jesus loved a little girl so much that He died for her and gave her a hope and a future. I now am fully aware of who I am. God is my Father, and heaven is my home! Being adopted once is very special, but being adopted twice is my greatest treasure.

Psalm 136(NLT)

Give thanks to the Lord, for He is good!
His faithful love endures forever.
Give thanks to the God of gods.
His faithful love endures forever.
Give thanks to the Lord of lords.
His faithful love endures forever.
Give thanks to Him who alone does mighty miracles.
His faithful love endures forever.

My Paraphrase of Psalm 136

Give thanks to Him who loved a single mother.
His faithful love endures forever.
Give thanks to Him for a mother's love for her unborn baby.
His faithful love endures forever.
Give thanks to Him for a Christian doctor.
His faithful love endures forever.
Give thanks to Him for a barren couple,
His faithful love endures forever.
Give thanks to Him for adoption.
His faithful love endures forever.
Give thanks to Him for tears of separation.
His faithful love endures forever.
Give thanks to Him for the love of a mom and dad.
His faithful love endures forever.
Give thanks to Him for salvation.
His faithful love endures forever.
Give thanks to Him for family.
His faithful love endures forever.
Give thanks to Him for orphans finding forever families.
His faithful love endures forever.
Give thanks to Him for brothers, sisters, and cousins,
His faithful love endures forever.
Give thanks to Him for a heavenly home.
His faithful love endures forever.
Give thanks to Him for tearful good-byes.
His faithful love endures forever.
Give thanks to Him for joyful reunions in heaven.
His faithful love endures forever.

Here is my first letter to my biological mother after our first phone conversation:

April 8, 1985

Dear Pauline,

The hardest thing about writing this letter is knowing how to address you. I guess Pauline will have to do for now, since that is the only name I knew you as.

My mom and dad have been so good to me. I had a wonderful childhood, but I guess deep down in my heart I always wondered who you are and what you look like. Whenever a special event happened in my life I wondered how you would have reacted ... if you would be proud, happy, etc. I've seen so many movies on TV about reunions of adopted children with their "blood relatives," and some of them were good endings and some were rather discouraging. As I mentioned on the phone, I tried to trace you several times but had no success. I'm so glad I finally found you!

I graduated from high school in 1976 at Bellaire High School in Michigan (approximately forty miles from Traverse City). In eleventh grade, I was crowned "Miss Bellaire," "Autumn Festival Queen," and was "Miss Congeniality" at the National Trout Festival. This was all because it was a small town. I'm telling you that because I often thought that would make you proud. Please don't start thinking I'm pretty or sophisticated—I'm not any of the above. Just very average. I'm 5'10," hazel eyes, dark brown hair (actually it's getting gray but I'm not letting it), and I've got a lot of freckles, especially after sunning.

Calle', my three year old daughter is blonde and blue-eyed. She resembles my husband's sisters. Charles, eight months, is looking like he'll have dark hair. Both our children were bald babies. Mom said I was bald until I was almost two. Then my hair came in dark and curly. I was a very shy little girl. In high school I became very people-orientated. Helping Mom and Dad in the church was good for me too. I played the coronet (like a trumpet) in school and was first chair. I loved being in the band. Also, I sang in the school and church choir. I can play the piano slightly, enough to get by. I love drawing and painting, although I haven't had much time to do either lately. I crochet, sew some clothes, and dabble in a few crafts. Now, besides working full-time with my husband who is pastoring a church, I travel to several churches in Wisconsin, Ohio, Illinois, Indiana, and Michigan, training church workers how to teach children more effectively. It's really exciting and a lot of fun. My husband and I have our hands full in the pastorate. We are now at a small country church of fifty people.

Oh yes, I went to Marion College for one year in 1977–78. Then I was married April 21, 1979. We went to Allentown, Pennsylvania, to college after that and we are now at our second church.

The picture I am sending is not recent. It was taken in July of 1982. I have shorter hair now. Do I resemble anybody? I'd love to know.

This letter really must sound jumbled but it's hard to gather my thoughts. I hope I might have answered some questions. Thank you for loving me so much to give me such wonderful parents. I love you too!

Linda

"You made all the delicate, inner parts of my body and knit them together in my mother's womb. Thank you for making me so wonderfully complex! It is amazing to think about. Your workmanship is marvelous—and how well I know it. You were there while I was being formed in utter seclusion! You saw me before I was born and scheduled each day of my life before I began to breathe. Every day was recorded in your book!"

Psalm 139:13-16 (NLT)

Printed in the United States
By Bookmasters